'Search Me, O God'

The Practice of Self-Examination

Andrew Atherstone

Curate, Christ Church, Abingdon

GROVE BOOKS LIMITED
RIDLEY HALL RD CAMBRIDGE CB3 9HU

Contents

Acknowledgments

I am grateful to Roly Riem for his comments on an early draft of this booklet. Bible quotations are taken from the New International Version.

The Cover Illustration is by Peter Ashton

First Impression November 2003
ISSN 0262-799X
ISBN 1 85174 545 9

A Forgotten Spiritual Discipline? 1

Look into your heart, as in a book, and see if you can read the same.

John Bunyan (1628–88)

'Self-examination' sounds like an intimate and embarrassing medical procedure, to be conducted in the privacy of one's bedroom. Public health organizations now advise us regularly to examine ourselves, to ensure our bodies have not developed any suspicious lumps or unusual growths. And if one is discovered we are to seek medical attention urgently.

But self-examination is also a spiritual discipline with a long Christian history. It involves examining not our bodies but our hearts (in the biblical sense —the centre of our inner personal lives) and our position before God. With the help of God's Spirit and God's Word, we search out areas of sin, leading to repentance, amendment of life and a renewed desire for holiness. The pursuit of holiness is, of course, a Christian priority. God is holy and calls his people to be holy (Leviticus 11.44). The evangelical author James Packer summarizes what this involves:

> Holiness is consecrated closeness to God. Holiness is in essence obeying God, living to God and for God, imitating God, keeping his law, taking his side against sin, doing righteousness, performing good works, following Christ's teaching and example, worshipping God in the Spirit, loving and serving God and men out of reverence for Christ. In relation to God, holiness takes the form of a single-minded passion to please by love and loyalty, devotion and praise. In relation to sin, it takes the form of a resistance movement, a discipline of not gratifying the desires of the flesh, but of putting to death the deeds of the body. Holiness is, in a word, God-taught, Spirit-wrought Christlikeness, the sum and substance of committed discipleship, the demonstration of faith working by love, the responsive outflow in righteousness of supernatural life from the hearts of those who are born again.[1]

Christians do not become holy by accident. Rather we need to fight against sin in our lives constantly and consciously, earnestly seeking the Holy Spirit's sanctifying work, and self-examination is part of that process. How can we tell where we fail to imitate God if we do not stop to scrutinize our actions and attitudes? How can we know where our passion to please him has gone cold, if we do not take time to observe our spiritual progress? How can we resist sin if we do not bother to consider which of our thoughts, words and deeds have been sinful?

Sadly, self-examination is much neglected by Christians today. This is particularly the case within Protestant evangelicalism. Authors in the Catholic tradition do address self-examination when writing about the spiritual life. For example, the Ignatian practice of 'Examen' (examination of conscience) has become well-known.[2] Yet in Protestant circles self-examination is seldom practised and even more seldom taught. It is difficult to find any recent treatment of this spiritual discipline from an evangelical perspective and reformed or charismatic preachers are generally silent on the subject.[3] Even a modern classic such as Richard Foster's *Celebration of Discipline* (1978) only mentions it in passing.

This was not always the case. For many centuries self-examination was a central part of holiness teaching within Protestant evangelicalism. It was widely advocated in the sixteenth century by the Reformers. For example, Martin Luther and Thomas Cranmer regularly examined their lives on the basis of the Ten Commandments and for this reason included the Commandments within their public liturgies. The Puritans were famous for their passion for holiness, and often mocked for it, as were the Wesleyans at the time of the eighteenth century Evangelical Revival. Both groups practised the daily discipline of self-examination with great diligence, as is evident from their spiritual autobiographies and surviving diaries. The journals of John Wesley and his circle, for instance, have been described as 'a Methodist's constant companion and conscience…a ledger of the soul and a mirror for the spirit, recording and reflecting the progress and pitfalls of his struggle to advance along the path of holy living.'[4] A similar emphasis is to be found in the published diaries of great evangelical role models such as David Brainerd, Henry Martyn, William Wilberforce and Edward Bickersteth. Self-examination was expounded in detail from the pulpit by prominent preachers such as Jonathan Edwards, James Haldane, Charles Spurgeon and J C Ryle, who urged it as a vital Christian duty. During the Victorian period, evangelical authors produced a plethora of pamphlets and devotional books on the topic as part of their wide-ranging concern to stimulate practical holiness.[5]

O, fellow-Christians! Let us cease to wonder why our heads are so full, and our hearts so cold—why our doctrine is so correct, and our experience so low—why our privileges are so highly estimated in words, and so little enjoyed in the heart—why our code of Christian morality is so good, and our tempers so unmortified—why the way to heaven is so clearly known, but our growth in the divine life so low…Let us cease to wonder, while we search not, probe not, sift not, and penetrate not more into the quick of our selfish, back-sliding, and unhumbled hearts. **A Victorian clergyman**

The following pages explain the biblical basis behind self-examination and the role of God's Spirit and God's Word in the process. They offer practical guidelines for beginning this spiritual discipline, with examples of appropriate prayers and questions for meditation. If we truly want to emulate the depth of holy living evident in previous generations of Christian saints, the rediscovery of self-examination is vital.

The Friend of Sinners

2

The examination of our hearts is an important spiritual discipline, but it is hardly a cheerful one.

Indeed it can be painful and difficult. Discovering the extent of sin in one's life is never an enjoyable experience. Throughout its pages, the Bible is pessimistic about our human nature and treats sin with deadly seriousness. Sin is rebellion against God. It is detestable to him and separates us from him. Scripture explains that all have rebelled and therefore all are guilty before God and facing his holy wrath. Sin brings sorrow and suffering to many people in this life and irretrievable ruin to some in the next. That is the bad news. It is a stark diagnosis and self-examination brings home to us the distressing reality of sin in our lives.

> For the first time I examined myself with a seriously practical purpose. And there I found what appalled me; a zoo of lusts, a bedlam of ambitions, a nursery of fears, a hareem of fondled hatreds. My name was legion. **C S Lewis (1898–1963)**

Thankfully the Bible does not stop with the bad news. It goes on to explain that no matter how terrible our sins, forgiveness can be obtained through the sin-bearing death of Jesus Christ, the Saviour of the world. This is the heart of the glorious Christian gospel—it is good news indeed. Throughout Jesus' earthly ministry we see that he is the Friend of sinners, always taking the initiative to seek out those who have rebelled against God and invite them back into relationship with him. This message comes across again and again in the New Testament, such as in the well-known 'comfortable words':

- 'Come to me, all who labour and are heavy laden, and I will give you rest'. (Matthew 11.28)
- 'God so loved the world that he gave his only-begotten Son, that whoever believes in him should not perish but have eternal life.' (John 3.16)
- 'This saying is true, and worthy of full acceptance, that Christ Jesus came into the world to save sinners' (1 Timothy 1.15).
- 'If anyone sins, we have an advocate with the Father, Jesus Christ the righteous; and he is the propitiation for our sins' (1 John 2.1–2).

Likewise the Old Testament offers vivid and wonderful expressions for the forgiveness of sins—they are blown away like a cloud (Isaiah 44.22); they are removed as far as the east is from the west (Psalm 103.12); they are trodden underfoot and hurled into the depths of the sea (Micah 7.19); they are put behind God's back (Isaiah 38.17) and forgotten by him (Jeremiah 31.34). This forgiveness and reconciliation with God is found when we repent of our wrongdoing and put our faith in Jesus Christ.

Self-examination is a chastening discipline. Yet its purpose is not to leave us despairing at our ingrained sinfulness, but to remind us to look with confidence to our gracious Saviour. Self-examination should lead to a renewed trust in Jesus Christ and a firmer dependence upon this Friend of sinners.

3 God the Searcher of Hearts

The Academy Awards ceremony ('the Oscars') in Hollywood has become a celebration of external beauty.

Those who walk the red carpet in front of the world's photographers and TV cameras spend hundreds of thousands of dollars upon the finest clothing, hairstyles, cosmetics and plastic surgery (face-lifts, liposuction and breast implants are increasingly *de rigeur*). Their greatest concern is with public image and outward impression.

God, however, looks for a purity which is more than skin deep. Jesus explained at the Sermon on the Mount that it is those who are 'pure *in heart*' who are blessed (Matthew 5.8). As the Puritans used to say, the heart of holiness is holiness in the heart. And God is not casual in assessing our internal, spiritual condition. He examines us, tests us, probes us. He is the Lord 'who searches hearts and minds' (Revelation 2.23, Psalm 7.9). Numerous examples from Scripture could be given:

- 'A man's ways are in full view of the Lord, and he examines all his paths' (Proverbs 5.21)
- 'The crucible for silver and the furnace for gold, but the Lord tests the heart' (Proverbs 17.3)
- 'The Lord searches every heart and understands every motive behind the thoughts' (1 Chronicles 28.9)
- 'I the Lord search the heart and examine the mind' (Jeremiah 17.10).

We may be reasonably successful at keeping our sins secret from other people, including our closest friends. We may even be able to hide them from ourselves. Yet God cannot be fooled. Queen Elizabeth I did not have 'a window into men's souls,' but God does. He sees straight into our hearts and we stand spiritually naked before him. As the Bible declares, 'Nothing in all creation is hidden from God's sight. Everything is uncovered and laid bare before the eyes of him to whom we must give account' (Hebrews 4.13).

This theme is explored in fear and wonder by King David in Psalm 139, where he outlines God's amazingly detailed knowledge of us:

O Lord, you have searched me and you know me.
You know when I sit and when I rise;
  you perceive my thoughts from afar.
You discern my going out and my lying down;
  you are familiar with all my ways.
Before a word is on my tongue
  you know it completely, O Lord.   Psalm 139.1–4

Much as he might like to run away, David realizes it is impossible to escape from God's presence. Even up in the heavens or in the depths of Sheol or on the far side of the ocean, the Lord is there. He cannot deceive God by hiding in the darkness, because 'even the darkness will not be dark to you' (v 12). As one author expresses it, 'God has infra-red vision; he sees in the night as he sees in the day.'[6]

The idea of a God who watches our every movement and reads our private thoughts may seem oppressive and even tyrannical—like the Orwellian nightmare, *Nineteen Eighty-four* (1949), with its constant reminder, 'Big Brother is watching you.' The all-embracing knowledge of God may seem a menacing threat, as if he were 'a master-detective who snoops like some insatiable nosey-parker into every detail of our existence, armed with x-ray cameras and laser probes.'[7] Certainly David's psalm is initially ambivalent. When he declares, 'You hem me in behind and before' (v 5), or asks, 'Where can I go from your Spirit?' (v 7), it is hard to tell whether he is complaining at feeling trapped or thanking God for his protection. Nevertheless David's over-riding emotion is one of gratitude—he praises his Creator, describing God's complete knowledge of him as 'too wonderful' (v 6) and 'precious' (v 17). He is not resentful at God's irresistible, all-seeing eyes, but considers them a comfort and reassurance. The psalmist approaches the Searcher of Hearts not as a hostile threat but a welcome refuge.

Francis Thompson's famous poem, *The Hound of Heaven* (1893), reflects the same contrast of emotions as Psalm 139. It is about someone running as fast as possible away from God:

> I fled Him, down the nights and down the days;
> I fled Him, down the arches of the years;
> I fled Him, down the labyrinthine ways
> Of my own mind, and in the midst of tears
> I hid from Him, and under running laughter.
> Up vistaed hopes I sped;
> And shot, precipitated,
> Adown titanic glooms of chasmèd fears,
> From those strong Feet that followed, followed after...

By the end of the poem, the fugitive is finally cornered by his Pursuer and surrounded in ominous darkness. Yet when he turns around in trepidation to face the Hound of Heaven, he discovers that 'my gloom, after all' was in fact the 'shade of His hand, outstretched caressingly.' The Hound of Heaven turns out to be not a threat, but a comfort.

Our response to the Lord's searching of our hearts depends, ultimately, on our relationship with him. As has been seen, two opposite reactions are possible. If we rebel against God and insist on living without reference to him, his knowledge of us bodes danger. Yet as soon as we repent and turn back to him, that knowledge becomes a sign of his merciful care for the intimate details of our lives.

> False peace is not willing to be tried. It is a sign they are bad wares which will not endure the light; a sign a man has stolen goods, when he will not have his house searched.   Thomas Watson (1620–86)

As the familiar Prayer of Preparation states, we approach 'Almighty God, to whom all hearts are open, all desires known, and from whom no secrets are hidden.' Moses recognized this: 'You have set our iniquities before you, our secret sins in the light of your presence' (Psalm 90.8). Our natural inclination is to run from God and hide our wrongdoing, but this is clearly futile. At the Fall, Adam and Eve's first response to their sin was to hide from the Lord among the trees of the garden of Eden. Yet the Lord sought them out—again, this could be a threat or comfort, a sign of judgment or grace, depending on our perspective (Genesis 3). When Achan stole plunder from Jericho and hid it away, the Lord saw and punished him (Joshua 7). When David seduced Bathsheba and secretly murdered her husband, the Lord saw and sent the prophet Nathan to rebuke the king (2 Samuel 12). When Ananias and Sapphira lied to the Holy Spirit and tried to deceive the Christian community, the Lord saw and struck them both dead (Acts 5). These are sobering foretastes of the final Day of Judgment, when there will be no more secrets. We will then be seen as we truly are. It will be a Day of acute embarrassment and condemnation for hypocrites who have spent their lives feigning holiness, as Jesus warned the Pharisees (Luke 12.2–3).

> Everyone should examine himself, so as to call himself to an account, and in a manner to summon himself before God's tribunal. We then see that men can never be brought to repentance, except they set their own evils before their eyes, so as to feel ashamed and to ask themselves, as it were in great fear, 'What have we done?'
> John Calvin (1509–64)

These awesome Bible truths should spur us on to forsake our sins and put our faith in Jesus Christ alone. When King David tried to hide his wrongdoing from God, he suffered inner turmoil, expressed in Psalm 32. At first he kept silent about his sin and attempted to cover it up, but found himself 'groaning all day long' because the Lord's 'hand was heavy upon me' (vv 3-4). When he decided to confess honestly, he met at last with forgiveness and relief (vv 1-2, 5). David discovered for himself the truth of the proverb, 'He who conceals his sins does not prosper, but whoever confesses and renounces them finds mercy' (Proverbs 28.13). We cannot hide our sins, so must repent of them and God will take them away. This is the wonderful paradox of honest confession. The sins we try to cover and conceal, God uncovers and reveals; the sins we uncover and confess, God covers and forgives.

4   'Examine Yourselves...'

The heart must be searched—searched to the very core. The deepest recesses of it must be sounded. Everyone should know how things are going on in his soul.   Ashton Oxenden (1808–92)

A superficial glance is not enough for a thing so deep, an unsteady view will not suffice for a thing so wavering, nor a casual look for a thing so deceitful as the human heart.   Hannah More (1745–1833)

There are numerous injunctions in the Bible for God's people to be diligent, alert and always watchful about their spiritual state. For example, God instructed the Israelites who were about to enter the Promised Land, 'be careful, and watch yourselves closely so that you do not forget the things your eyes have seen or let them slip from your heart as long as you live' (Deuteronomy 4.9). Likewise, on the eve of his crucifixion, Jesus told his friends, 'Watch and pray so that you will not fall into temptation' (Matthew 26.41). This theme is picked up in the New Testament letters, where Paul writes, 'Be very careful how you live' (Ephesians 5.15). Peter insists, 'Be self-controlled and alert' (1 Peter 5.8). Elsewhere we read, 'Above all else, guard your heart, for it is the well-spring of your life' (Proverbs 4.23).

Part of what is involved in being 'watchful' is frequent examination of our hearts and our spiritual state before God. Paul explicitly commands the church at Corinth, 'Examine yourselves to see whether you are in the faith; test yourselves' (2 Corinthians 13.5). Is our profession of faith true? Are we living as God's redeemed people? What particular areas of sin in our lives need to be confessed and forsaken? Similarly, after the destruction of Jerusalem, Jeremiah exhorted the survivors, 'Let us examine our ways and test them, and let us return to the Lord' (Lamentations 3.40).

Various images from everyday life help to illustrate aspects of self-examination:

School Pupils are often examined by their teachers to see whether they are making progress in their studies. This may be by regular weekly tests or lengthy examinations at the end of each term. The questions asked are always varied, to keep students on their toes. In the same way, the self-examiner asks difficult questions of her heart and life to see whether she is making progress in her Christian discipleship.

Hospital In a comprehensive medical check-up, the doctor thoroughly examines her patient—blood pressure, brain scan, X-ray, cholesterol and other important tests. This can be painful, but is beneficial in the long-run. Sometimes a serious illness is discovered which requires urgent treatment. In the same way, the self-examiner searches out areas of disease in his inner life. It is better to have a truthful diagnosis, however stark, than live in ignorance of our true state.

Law Court The accused stands in the witness box while a barrister cross-examines him. His statements, actions and motives are tested in order to discover the truth. In the same way, the self-examiner scrutinizes her heart. Our hearts, by nature, are like dishonest witnesses who aim to deceive and need to be questioned closely by a shrewd lawyer.

Shop Coins paid over the shop-counter will be happily accepted without much attention. However, if a customer tries to purchase goods with a £50 note, the shop-keeper will suddenly become alert and study it closely. It would be disastrous for his business if such a large sum of money later turned out to be forged. In the same way, close examination of our hearts and lives is vital because our position before God is a matter of eternal importance.

To have a flourishing estate and a mind in disorder; to keep exact accounts with a Steward and no reckoning with our Maker; to have an accurate knowledge of loss or gain in our business and to remain utterly ignorant whether our spiritual concerns are improving or declining; to be cautious in ascertaining at the end of every year how much we have increased or diminished our fortune and to be careless whether we have incurred profit or loss in faith and holiness, is making a wretched estimate of the comparative value of things.
Hannah More (1745–1833)

Expedition When a cartographer is mapping out a new country she does not simply walk down the main roads and visit the major cities. Instead she examines every possible square mile, climbing every mountain and hill, visiting the smallest hamlet, tracing the forest track and stream. If it is a thorough geological survey she even examines the rocks and soil. Charles Spurgeon, the Baptist preacher, takes up this image of exploration when speaking of self-examination:

> Now, do the same with your heart. 'Examine yourselves.' Go right through yourselves from the beginning to the end. Stand not only on the mountains of your public character, but go into the deep valleys of your private life. Be not content to sail on the broad river of your outward actions, but go follow back the narrow rill till you discover your secret motive. Look not only at your performance, which is but the product of the soil, but dig into your heart and examine the vital principle.[8]

If possible, time should regularly be set aside for extended self-examination, particularly on Sundays (especially before the Lord's Supper), at significant points in one's life (such as birthdays, anniversaries or New Year) and during penitential seasons (Advent and Lent). However, briefer self-examination is invaluable as part of our daily devotions, perhaps a few minutes each evening to reflect upon the past day and to repent of our sins. For example, it has been John Stott's habit for many years to reflect daily upon the Spirit's nine-fold fruit and pray for more of their appearance in his life.[9]

> Do with your hearts as you do with your watches, wind them up every morning by prayer, and at night examine whether your hearts have gone true all day, whether the wheels of your affections have moved swiftly to heaven.   Thomas Watson (1620–86)

Of course, like any spiritual discipline, self-examination can be overdone as well as underdone, in which case it becomes morbid and perfunctory. When driving a car, we may check before each journey that there is enough petrol in the tank and that the tyres have not gone flat. Yet we do not stop the car every two miles to look under the bonnet and conduct a full MOT test. Having said this, full MOT tests are important and our spiritual lives require them at frequent intervals.

Self-Examination Before the Lord's Supper

The Bible explicitly commands self-examination before the Lord's Supper. The apostle Paul explained at length to the church at Corinth that this was vital for both their spiritual and physical health:

> ...whoever eats the bread or drinks the cup of the Lord in an unworthy manner will be guilty of sinning against the body and blood of the Lord. A man ought to examine himself before he eats of the bread and drinks of the cup. For anyone who eats and drinks without recognizing the body of the Lord eats and drinks judgment on himself. That is why many among you are weak and sick, and a number of

> you have fallen asleep. But if we judged ourselves, we would not
> come under judgment. 1 Corinthians 11.27–31

As a result of this warning, liturgies for Holy Communion often include an emphasis upon self-examination leading to repentance. For example, the 1662 *Book of Common Prayer* exhorts communicants

> ...to search and examine your own consciences (and that not lightly, and after the manner of dissemblers with God; but so) that ye may come holy and clean to such a heavenly Feast...to examine your lives and conversations by the rule of God's commandments; and where-insoever ye shall perceive yourselves to have offended, either by will, word, or deed, there to bewail your own sinfulness, and to confess yourselves to Almighty God, with full purpose of amendment of life...

Common Worship includes a similar, though much abbreviated, exhortation: 'As we gather at the Lord's table we must recall the promises and warnings given to us in the Scriptures and so examine ourselves and repent of our sins...' Since there are usually only a few quiet minutes (if any) during public worship, self-scrutiny is best begun in private at home before attendance at Holy Communion.

'Search me, O God': Convicted by God's Spirit

5

> What a sink of corruption is the heart! And yet I can go from day to day in self-seeking and self-pleasing! Lord, show me myself...Reveal to me the evil of my heart, O thou heart-searching God.
> Journal of Henry Martyn (1781–1812)

'Self-examination' is, in one sense, a misnomer. It sounds no different from self-assessment or self-audit in the secular world, an act of sheer human determination from which God is excluded. Christian self-examination is a discipline, but it is distinctly a *spiritual* discipline. Perhaps it therefore ought to be re-named 'Submitting to examination by the Holy Spirit.' The heart of true self-examination is to invite the Holy Spirit to search us. The Spirit is our strong ally in the battle for holiness.

At the end of his long meditation on God's omniscience in Psalm 139, King David does not try to maintain his privacy but instead invites the Lord to examine him completely:

> Search me, O God, and know my heart;
>   test me and know my anxious thoughts.
> See if there is any offensive way in me,
>   and lead me in the way everlasting.   Psalm 139.23–24

Elsewhere David prays in similar fashion: 'Test me, O Lord, and try me, examine my heart and my mind' (Psalm 26.2). In these instances he is not inviting God to search his heart for God's own benefit. Of course he is aware that God already knows him totally. Rather, the king wants to be scrutinized by God in order to be shown the results of that scrutiny. Instead of clinging proudly to his independence, he submits to the Lord's searching without reluctance, welcoming God's involvement in his life.

This plea has been movingly expressed in a little-known hymn by Frank Bottome (1823–94), an American Methodist pastor:

> Search me, O God, my actions try,
> And let my life appear
> As seen by thine all-searching eye;
> To mine my ways make clear.
>
> Search all my sense and know my heart,
> Who only canst make known,
> And let the deep, the hidden part,
> To me be fully shown.
>
> Throw light into the darkened cells
> Where passion reigns within;
> Quicken my conscience till it feels
> The loathsomeness of sin.
>
> Search all my thoughts, the secret springs,
> The motives that control,
> The chambers where polluted things
> Hold empire o'er the soul.
>
> Search, till thy fiery glance has cast
> Its holy light through all,
> And I by grace am brought at last
> before thy face to fall.

Without the aid of the Holy Spirit, self-examination becomes a mere self-delusion. There are three main reasons why, without God's help, it is impossible to come to a true knowledge of ourselves.

1 Our Sin No Longer Shocks Us

It is easy to grow so de-sensitized to our sin that we fail to see its true horror. God hates sin (see, for example, Psalm 5.4–6, Proverbs 6.16–19), yet the more familiar we are with our moral corruption the more we put up with it. We are no longer hurt, grieved or shocked by the sin which is ingrained in us. Our hearts are quickly hardened and we become blasé.

Oscar Wilde's novel, *The Picture of Dorian Gray* (1891), is a disturbing account of a handsome young man who one day wishes that his painted portrait would grow old and ugly while he would retain his good looks forever. Dorian's early innocence quickly vanishes and as the years pass he leads a life progressively more corrupt, characterized by obscene language, drunkenness, promiscuity and even murder. Strangely, while all around him grow older, Dorian remains as youthful and handsome as he ever was. Yet he has a terrible secret—hidden in the attic is that portrait, the image of which reflects the state of his heart. It has become a gruesome and repulsive sight. In a similar way, we need to be shown the true horror of our sin from God's perspective—what we are really like on the inside. Only thus will we be shaken out of our spiritual complacency and recapture a holy hatred of evil. As Somerset Maugham once said, 'If I wrote down every thought I have ever thought, and every deed I have ever done, people would call me a monster of depravity.'

2 We Are Prejudiced in Our Own Favour

> Selfishness disposes us to over-rate our good qualities and to overlook or extenuate our defects...The corruption of human nature clouds our moral sight and blunts our moral sensibility...Doubtless the perfect purity of the Supreme Being makes him see in us stains far more in number and deeper in dye than we ourselves can discover.
> William Wilberforce (1759–1833)

It is humiliating to see ourselves as we truly are and our pride rebels. We invent excuses to persuade ourselves that our sinful lifestyle is not in fact sinful. We adopt euphemisms to describe wickedness—lies become 'economy with the truth' or 'spin,' stealing becomes 'borrowing' and adultery becomes merely 'a fling.' Although we can easily see the speck of sawdust in our neighbour's eye, we avoid the plank of wood in our own (Matthew 7.1–5). Our prejudiced judgment is not to be trusted. As the prophet Jeremiah observes, 'The heart is deceitful above all things and beyond cure. Who can understand it?' (Jeremiah 17.9). Our self-justification leads to self-deception, which is disastrous for our spiritual health.

3 Satan Tries to Deceive Us

Satan is the 'prince of darkness' and the 'father of lies,' the master of delusion. He wants to blind us to the true state of our hearts. With the serpent's cunning, he attempts to beguile us and sear our consciences. He would persuade us that we are in no particular danger from sin and that we are holier than we really are.

> How difficult a task it is to read one's own heart—how impossible is thorough self-examination without the aid of the Spirit. In looking back on the past week, the Tempter brings all that I have striven to do for God into bold relief, but casts a cloud over my many many short-comings. But that which appears so fair and beautiful, when honestly examined is found to hide a mass of deformity.
>
> Journal of Francis Chavasse (1846–1928)

Faced with these difficulties, it is impossible to see the true state of our hearts without God's help. Therefore self-examination should always be conducted in an attitude of prayer and begin with an invitation for the Holy Spirit to show us our sin and make us sorry for it. As Jesus declares, it is the special role of the Spirit to 'convict the world of guilt in regard to sin and righteousness and judgment' (John 16.8). This is seen, for instance, when the Spirit is poured out on the Day of Pentecost and the gathered crowd are convicted of their sins and 'cut to the heart' (Acts 2.37).

It is impossible to see the true state of our hearts without God's help

Of course the Holy Spirit can convict us of our wrongdoing at any time, in any place. This might be during a specifically 'religious' event, such as listening to a sermon in church or to a Christian band at a music festival. Or it might be 'out of the blue,' when we least expect it—wandering around an art gallery or reading a letter or walking past a shop or watching TV or almost any other imaginable scenario. The Holy Spirit will not be limited to speak merely at our invitation. However, it is still important to set aside a focussed time when we can actively welcome the Spirit's scrutiny of us and listen intently to what he would say about the state of our hearts. This is the aim of self-examination.

When the living-room curtains are drawn back on a sunny morning and light streams in, things are revealed which were not visible in the darkness of the previous evening. Although the room had seemed spotless, it now becomes possible to see dust on top of the bookcases, crumbs on the carpet and cob-webs in the corners. If the sunlight is particularly bright, particles can even be seen floating in what was assumed to be 'pure' air. In the same way, when we allow the Holy Spirit to shine upon the darkest recesses of our hearts, he shows us our sin. In one of the paradoxes of the Christian life, the holier we become (as the Holy Spirit works upon us) the more we realize how unholy we are.

'Sharper Than Any Double-edged Sword': Judged by God's Word 6

By what standards shall we measure our personal holiness, with the Holy Spirit's help? There are three possibilities, the first two of which are popular but foolish.

1 Our Own Standards

Our natural inclination is to make up our own rules about holiness and judge ourselves accordingly. Often we only aim at what we already achieve and thus become conceited. Yet the Bible warns against those 'who are wise in their own eyes and clever in their own sight' (Isaiah 5.21). In Corinth, Paul pointed out the absurdity of the arrogant 'super-apostles':

> When they measure themselves by themselves and compare themselves with themselves, they are not wise...For it is not the one who commends himself who is approved, but the one whom the Lord commends. 2 Corinthians 10.12, 18

2 The World's Standards

It is often the virtues promoted by our circles of friends which we consider important. We adopt the moral values of society and are especially satisfied if we appear holier than most other people. Yet it is not safe to judge ourselves by the world's standards. As Jesus warned the self-righteous Pharisees, 'You are the ones who justify yourselves in the eyes of men, but God knows your hearts. What is highly valued among men is detestable in God's sight' (Luke 16.15).

3 God's Standards

> Everyone should examine his own life, and compare not only his actions, but also his thoughts, with that perfect rule of righteousness which is laid down in the law...The more diligently anyone examines himself, the more readily will he acknowledge that if God should discover our secret faults, there would be found in us an abyss of sins so great as to have neither bottom nor shore. John Calvin (1509–64)

In a heavily guarded vault in a chateau at Sèvres near Paris is a solid cylinder of platinum-iridium alloy maintained at constant temperature —the world's official standard for the kilogram. It is held by the Bureau International des Poids et Mesures whose task is to ensure the accurate implementation of the metric system. If there is any dispute about what constitutes a true kilogram, the Sèvres prototype provides the answer. Yet even this system is not completely infallible. Like the Imperial Standard yard before it, the kilogram has reportedly shrunk over the years—by fifty micrograms, about the weight of a grain of sand.

God's standard for holiness is laid down in the Bible, and unlike the official kilogram it is uneroded. If Christians have any dispute about what constitutes genuine holy living, we turn to the Scriptures to adjudicate. Only there do we find a true test for our character. The Ten Commandments, for instance, encapsulate God's requirements for righteousness. These are expounded and applied at length by the prophets and apostles, worked out in the lives of godly men and women from Bible history, and completely fulfilled by Jesus Christ himself. God's standards for holiness do not change, any more than God himself changes.

God's standards for holiness do not change, any more than God himself changes

Therefore a vital part of self-examination is to soak ourselves in the Scriptures and meditate prayerfully upon them. God's Word is 'useful for teaching, rebuking, correcting and training in righteousness' (2 Timothy 3.16). We do not sit in judgment upon the Bible, but it upon us. Like a sharp sword, it cuts deeply to the darkest corners of our inner life and lays bare spiritual realities we would rather keep hidden. God's Word does not just judge religious observance or outward morality—instead 'it judges the thoughts and attitudes of the heart' (Hebrews 4.12).

> It is as troublesome for sinners to look into themselves to examine their lives as it is for men whose business is declining to look into their books and cast up their accounts.   Ralph Venning (1620–73)

Law or Gospel?

Self-examination, if distorted or misunderstood, can turn into legalism. A constant focus upon the details of holy living sometimes results in the mistaken view that we earn God's favour by keeping his standards. This leads either to Pharisaical self-righteousness or abject despondency. The plain fact is that no one is able to keep God's righteous standards, as revealed in his Word, because he demands 100% of obedience 100% of the time. As someone has said, 'It is like carrying a sheet of fragile glass—one slip and it is shattered.'[10] Likewise the apostle James declares, 'whoever keeps the whole law and yet stumbles at just one point is guilty of breaking all of it' (James 2.10). It is impossible to earn God's favour by living holy lives, because no one is without sin, except Christ himself.

During self-examination it is important to remember that the Bible's rules about righteousness are given not to save us but to show us our need of a Saviour. They expose our sin and reveal how corrupt and rebellious we truly are. No one can meditate upon the Ten Commandments, for example, without concluding, 'I've failed and I need Jesus to save me.' This is argued at greatest length by Paul in his letters to the Romans and the Galatians, where he explains that we are justified by faith alone, through Christ alone, and not by observing the law. He states:

- 'No one will be declared righteous in God's sight by observing the law; rather, through the law we become conscious of sin.' (Romans 3.20)
- 'I would not have known what sin was except through the law.' (Romans 7.7)
- 'The law was put in charge to lead us to Christ that we might be justified by faith.' (Galatians 3.24)

We will not appreciate our need of Christ until we have first been shown the true state of our hearts and our guilt before God. John Stott expresses this well:

Not until the law has bruised and smitten us will we admit our need of the gospel to bind up our wounds. Not until the law has arrested and imprisoned us will we pine for Christ to set us free. Not until the law has condemned and killed us will we call upon Christ for justification and life. Not until the law has driven us to despair of ourselves will we ever believe in Jesus. Not until the law has humbled us even to hell will we turn to the gospel to raise us to heaven.[11]

The right response to being convicted of sin during self-examination is not to work harder to earn God's favour, but to thank him for sending Jesus as a Saviour. We seek holiness not as a means to salvation but in response to God's saving grace. Christians live under grace not law.

7 Repentance

Christians are called to a life of habitual repentance, as an integral part of holy living. The process of repentance has been usefully summarized as follows:

- realistic recognition that one has disobeyed and failed God
- regretful remorse at the dishonour one has done to God
- reverent requesting of God's pardon, cleansing of conscience, and help not to lapse in the same way again
- resolute renunciation of the sins in question, with deliberate thought of how to keep clear of them and live right for the future
- requisite restitution to any who have suffered material loss through one's wrongdoing.[12]

Self-examination, if properly conducted, should lead to such repentance. As has been seen earlier in this booklet, we have a gracious Friend of sinners who welcomes us into relationship with him and delights when we turn from our wrongdoing. When we repent and put our faith in Jesus Christ we find forgiveness and reconciliation with God. Thus self-examination is not about morbid introspection, but should cause us to 'fix our eyes on Jesus' (Hebrews 12.2).

8 Putting it into Practice

There is no fixed method for self-examination, but some general guiding principles may be helpful:

- set time aside
- pray for the help of God's Spirit
- meditate upon God's Word, asking in particular what it says

—about God's character and purposes
—about practical holy living
—about the opportunities and temptations you face today
- scrutinize your conduct and motives, including in the following areas:
  —your eternal position before God (are you 'in the faith'?)
  —your spiritual life (prayer, Bible reading, evangelism, church involvement)
  —your physical life (appetites, addictions, sex, recreation)
  —your family (spouse, children, parents)
  —your work (employees, boss, colleagues, competitors)
  —your community (neighbours, society)
  —your possessions (money, property, material things)
  —your time
  —your ambitions
- be honest with yourself and God
- identify your sins, especially your recurring or 'besetting' sins
- repent and confess your sins, being not vague but specific
- pray for increased personal holiness
- rely on the saving grace of Jesus Christ

Some also find it helpful to

- keep a journal, writing down the results of self-examination
- make specific resolutions for the future

My object in making this Journal is to accustom myself to self-examination, and to give my experience a visible form, so as to leave a stronger impression on the memory, and thus to improve my soul in holiness; for the review of such a lasting testimony will serve the double purpose of conviction and consolation.

Journal of Henry Martyn (1781–1812)

During self-examination there are also pit-falls on every side to be carefully avoided:

- *formalism:* vary the Bible passage you read and the questions you ask of your heart and life.
- *haste:* consider a few questions in detail, allowing time for serious reflection, rather than many superficially.
- *legalism:* remember that we are saved by grace through faith in Christ, not by observing the law.
- *self-righteousness:* if you think you have come anywhere near to

meeting God's standards for holy living, think again!
- *self-condemnation:* 'conviction' and 'condemnation' should not be confused. In Romans 7, Paul is convicted of his sin as he examines his life against God's holy law. Yet he can begin Romans 8: 'there is now no condemnation for those who are in Christ Jesus, because through Christ Jesus the law of the Spirit of life set me free from the law of sin and death.'
- *morbidness:* do not rake over old sins that have already been confessed and forsaken. Take confidence in the Bible's promises that sins of which we have repented have already been forgiven and forgotten by God.
- *introspection:* look faithfully to Christ; do not navel-gaze.

In conclusion, self-examination is a vital, practical discipline for the Christian believer. It is a painful process as we come face to face with the sin ingrained in our lives, yet is of tremendous spiritual benefit. With the aid of God's Spirit and God's Word we are led to heartfelt repentance, amendment of life and renewed reliance upon the saving grace of Jesus Christ. As we put this neglected spiritual discipline into frequent action, so by God's mercy we will begin to take precious steps forward along the path of Christ-like holy living.

Examples of prayers before and after self-examination and questions to ask of our hearts and lives are offered below. Many others could be given, but these provide a starting point and useful model.

Prayers Before Self-Examination

Holy, holy, holy Lord God Almighty,
you search my heart and examine my inmost thoughts.
I ask you now to help me in searching my own heart and life.
Enable me to judge myself by the standard of your Holy Word.
By your Holy Spirit show me the true state of my soul,
give me repentance for all my past sins,
heartfelt faith in Jesus Christ, the only Saviour from sin,
and deep humility before you,
for Jesus Christ's sake.
Amen.

Adapted from Edward Bickersteth (1786–1850)

Lord Jesus Christ, who sits at the right hand of the Father,
you are exalted as Prince and Saviour,
to give repentance and forgiveness of sins.

I come to you now for these blessings.
My heart is hard and impenitent
and little concerned by my sinfulness.
Give me that broken and contrite heart which God does not despise.
By your Holy Spirit, show me myself,
and bring me back to your heavenly Father and mine.
Returning to him, may I obtain mercy
and find that he does abundantly pardon.
Amen.

Adapted from Edward Bickersteth (1786–1850)

Questions During Self-Examination

The Ten Commandments (Exodus 20.1–17)

You shall have no other gods before me
- Do I love God with all my heart, mind, soul and strength?
- Is following God my absolute top priority?
- Do I acknowledge that Jesus Christ is the only way to God?
- Do I give my worship exclusively to the true and living God?
- Am I zealous for God's glory?

You shall not make for yourself an idol
- Where do I look for comfort or pleasure?
- Would I give up everything for God (possessions, career, family, health)?
- Do I try to make God in my own image?
- Have I distorted God's good gifts into idols?
- Am I enslaved by false thinking or the world's lies about money, sex and power?

You shall not misuse the name of the Lord your God
- Do I always remember the privilege of knowing God's name?
- Do I have a personal, intimate relationship with God?
- Do I honour and revere God?
- Am I offended when God's name is dishonoured?
- Do I seek to give glory to God with my words and actions?

Remember the Sabbath day by keeping it holy
- Do I thank God for the blessing of work?
- Am I obsessed by work? Does it consume my time, energy and thoughts?
- Do I set aside one full day a week to rest?
- Do I find my value in what I achieve or who I am in Christ?
- Do I trust God to provide even if I work less?

Honour your father and your mother
- Do I put effort into family relationships?
- Do I value and respect my parents? How do I express this?
- Do I listen to my parents' wisdom or despise it?
- Do I support my parents as they grow older?
- Am I the sort of parent that my children will want to honour?

You shall not murder
- Do I highly value all human life?
- Am I ever violent or abusive?
- How do I respond when I am humiliated, insulted or treated unfairly?
- Am I grieved by my unrighteous anger? Do I ever go to sleep angry?
- Am I quick to forgive, or do I hold grudges and seek revenge?
- Do I silently condone abortion or 'assisted suicide'?

You shall not commit adultery
- Do I treat sex as a precious, holy gift from God?
- If single, am I sexually abstinent? If married, am I faithful?
- Do I flirt?
- Is my thought-life pure? Do I dwell on sexual images or look at others lustfully?
- Do I resist the temptation of pornography (in films, books, magazines, the internet)?

You shall not steal
- Do I hate greed?
- Have I acquired things (however small) which rightly belong to others?
- Am I strictly honest when it comes to money (tax, loans, debts, expenses)? Am I quick to pay what I owe?
- Do I put in the hours at work?
- Do I cultivate a habit of generous giving?

You shall not give false testimony
- Do I speak only what is true, shunning exaggeration and 'spin'?
- Do I gossip? Do I flatter?
- Am I a person of my word? Do I keep my promises?
- Do I face the truth about myself, or hide behind masks and pretence?

You shall not covet
- Am I ever jealous or envious of others?
- Does God or the world shape my desires?
- Do I rejoice with thankfulness at the ways God has blessed me?
- Am I content in every situation?
- Do I practise generosity?

The Beatitudes (Matthew 5.1–12)

Am I poor in spirit?
- Do I feel my spiritual bankruptcy before God?
- Do I fight my spiritual pride?
- Am I acquainted with the depravity of my own evil heart?
- Do I receive the kingdom of heaven as an utterly undeserved gift?

Do I mourn for sin?
- Do I experience bitter sorrow at my repeated transgressions?
- Am I grieved by the world's evil?
- Do I truly appreciate the eternal consequences of sin?
- Do I rely on Christ alone for comfort?

Am I meek?
- Am I humble towards others, refusing to bully or domineer?
- Do I resist my lust for status and public recognition?
- Am I patient in the midst of difficulties?
- Do I gladly submit to God's will?

Do I hunger and thirst for righteousness?
- Do I realize my desperate lack of Christ-likeness?
- Do I have a consuming passion to be holy?
- Am I eager to be free from the power and pollution of sin?
- Do I actively promote righteousness in society?

Am I merciful?
- Am I quick to forgive or do I bear grudges?
- Do I share Christ's compassion for those in need?
- Am I actively involved in trying to relieve the miseries of others?
- Do I seek out the poor, the sick and the outcast?

Am I pure in heart?
- Am I whole-hearted in my devotion to God?
- Do I flee all temptations to impurity?
- Am I concerned for heart-righteousness rather than religious observance?
- Am I utterly sincere, with no deceit or pretence?

Am I a peacemaker?
- Do I bring friends to Christ, that they might find peace with God?
- Am I quick to promote harmony, avoiding all dissensions?
- Do I actively seek to unite those who are divided?
- Do I work for reconciliation between communities, families and churches?

Am I persecuted because of righteousness?
- Is the only offence I give because of my loyalty to Christ?
- Is my lifestyle distinctive for holiness?
- Do I rejoice with gladness at persecution and slander against me?
- Am I seeking an earthly or a heavenly reward?

The Gospel (Romans 1.16–18)

- Am I humbled before God's grace and holiness?
- Have I deeply felt my corruption and guilt before God, deserving his wrath?
- Am I grieved by my sin?
- Do I recognize the danger I am in without Christ?
- Do I recognize my inability to save myself or am I trying to earn merit with God?
- Do I know and believe that the gospel is the only way of salvation?
- Do I rely on Jesus Christ as my only Saviour?
- Have I actually turned from my sin and put my faith in Christ?
- Am I seeking righteousness as a gift from God?
- Am I truly grateful to God for saving me?
- Do I show this by a desire to be holy and please him in all things?
- Am I ever ashamed of the gospel? Do I stand up for the gospel in all situations?

Love (1 Corinthians 13)

- Do I count love as the best and greatest gift?
- Are my life and relationships characterized by self-sacrificial love?
- Do I imitate the love of Christ?
- Am I patient and long-suffering?
- Am I kind? Do I 'go the extra mile'?
- Am I envious or do I celebrate when good things happen to others?
- Am I boastful? Am I puffed up with my own importance?
- Am I proud?
- Am I rude?
- Am I self-seeking? Do I demand my rights and put my own interests first?
- Am I easily angered? Do I look for the best in other people or magnify their weaknesses?
- Do I keep a record of wrongs, or am I quick to forgive?
- Do I reject evil and rejoice when truth prevails?
- Do I always protect, always trust, always hope, always persevere?
- Am I grieved that I show so little of this love?
- Is it my constant aim to possess more of this great gift that never fails? Do I pray for it and work at it?
- Do I thank Christ for his overwhelming love for me—a love shown by his willingness to die on the cross for my sake?

Earthly and Heavenly Wisdom (James 3.13–18)

- Where am I looking for wisdom—to God or to the world's ideas?
- Do I deny the truth of God's Word through my actions?
- Do I harbour bitter envy or selfish ambition?
- Am I overly concerned for my position, my dignity, my rights?

- Do I contribute to disorder, hurt or division?
- Am I humble or inclined to boast?
- Am I pure, like Jesus Christ?
- Am I peace-loving?
- Am I considerate, gracious, tolerant?
- Am I submissive and teachable?
- Am I full of mercy and good fruit?
- Am I compassionate and quick to forgive?
- Am I impartial or double-minded?
- Am I sincere? Does my private life match my public image?
- Do I earnestly desire righteousness?
- Can God's wisdom be seen in the way I live my life?

The Christian Graces (2 Peter 1.3–7)
- Am I seeking to live by God's power or in my own strength?
- Do I receive God's promises in the Bible as trustworthy and true?
- Do I treat them as very great and precious?
- Have they changed my heart?
- Have they led me to flee the corruption in the world and all evil desires?
- Have I put my faith in Jesus Christ alone for salvation?
- Am I making every effort to add to my faith in all Christian graces?
- Have I added Christ-like goodness? Do I demonstrate this by my actions?
- Have I added knowledge? Do I read, think and discuss as a Christian?
- Have I added self-control? Do I restrain my natural appetites and desires?
- Have I added perseverance? Do I keeping going despite difficulties and opposition?
- Have I added godliness? Do I walk closely with Christ?
- Have I added brotherly kindness? Do I show care for my fellow Christians?
- Have I added love? Do I love as Christ loves?

Confessions After Self-Examination

Lord God,
I have sinned against you;
I have done evil in your sight.
I am sorry and repent, in particular of _____
Have mercy on me according to your love.
Wash away my wrongdoing and cleanse me from my sin.
Renew a right spirit within me
and restore me to the joy of your salvation,
through Jesus Christ my Lord.
Amen.   Adapted from *Common Worship*

O most mighty God, merciful Father,
who has compassion on all people and hates nothing you have made,
who does not desire the death of a sinner,
but rather that we should turn from our sin and be saved,
mercifully forgive my wrongdoing.
In particular I repent of _____
I am grieved and weighed down with the burden of my sins:
receive and comfort me.
Your nature is always to have mercy,
only you can forgive sins.
Spare me, good Lord, who you have redeemed,
do not bring your servant into judgment.
I acknowledge my wickedness and truly repent of my sin:
turn your anger from me and come quickly to save me,
that I may live with you forever,
through Jesus Christ my Lord.
Amen.   Adapted from the *Book of Common Prayer*

Notes

1   James Packer, *Keep in Step with the Spirit* (Leicester, 1995, new edition) pp 96–97.
2   *The Spiritual Exercises*, 24–44. According to Ignatius, the General Examen should include five steps:
    i)   to give thanks to God our Lord for the benefits I have received from him
    ii) to ask grace to know my sins and rid myself of them
    iii) to ask an account of my soul from the hour of rising to the present examen, hour by hour or
         period by period, first as to thoughts, then words, then deeds
    iv) to ask pardon of God our Lord for my faults
    v)   to resolve, with his grace, to amend them.
    See further, Donald St Louis, 'The Ignatian Examen' in Philip Sheldrake (ed), *The Way of Ignatius
    Loyola: Contemporary Approaches to* The Spiritual Exercises (London, 1991) pp 154–164; Margaret
    Hebblethwaite, *Way of St Ignatius: Finding God in All Things* (London, 1999, new edition) pp 126–148.
3   An honourable exception is James Packer, *A Passion for Holiness* (Nottingham, 1992).
4   Richard Heitzenrater (ed), *Diary of an Oxford Methodist: Benjamin Ingham, 1733–1734* (Durham, North
    Carolina, 1985) p 2.
5   For a survey of Victorian teaching on self-examination, see Andrew Atherstone (ed), 'Francis
    Chavasse's Undergraduate Diary 1865–68' in *Church of England Record Society* vol 12 (forthcoming,
    2004).
6   Roy Clements, *Songs of Experience* (Fearn, Ross-shire, 1993) p 173.
7   *ibid*, pp 170–171.
8   Charles Spurgeon, 'Self-examination' in *The New Park Street Pulpit*, vol 4 (1858).
9   Timothy Dudley-Smith, *John Stott: A Global Ministry* (Leicester, 2001) p 451.
10 Roy Clements, *No Longer Slaves: Set Free by Christ* (Leicester, 1997) p 49.
11 John Stott, *The Message of Galatians: Only One Way* (Leicester, 1992, new edition) p 93.
12 Packer, *Passion for Holiness*, pp 123–125.